Hypsilophodon

Written by Ron Wilson
Illustrated by Doreen Edwards

Library of Congress Cataloging in Publication Data

Wilson, Ron, 1941-
  Hypsilophodon.

  (The New dinosaur library)
  Summary: Introduces the hypsilophodon, one of the smaller ornithoscian, or bird-hipped, dinosaurs, a plant-eater believed to have been one of the fastest-running creatures ever to live on the earth.
  1. Hypsilophodon—Juvenile literature.
[1. Hypsilophodon.   2. Dinosaurs]   I. Title.   II. Series.
QE862.O65W55   1984   567.9'7   84-11489
ISBN 0-86592-205-5

Rourke Enterprises, Inc.
Vero Beach, FL 32964

Diplodocus

Pteranodon

Woolly Mammoth

Hypsilophodon

Allosaurus

Hypsilophodon

Ichthyosaurus

The young Hypsilophodons had been behind the rock for several hours. In fact since the sun went down. They had slept only for short periods. Several days before they had been driven out by their parents. This was the normal way of things. With their own adult groups there was never enough room for the young as well. Homeless, the young Hypsilophodons had endeavored to find new territory. So far their search had been in vain. Each time they had stopped they had been driven away.

The creatures were very restless. A few slept, but most were awake. One Hypsilophodon stood guard. They took turns sleeping, but this system didn't seem to work well. The Hypsilophodons were waiting for daylight. At least then they could see what was happening. They were also hungry. Perhaps it was the hunger pangs which kept some of the creatures awake.

At the moment there was no noise except for the occasional faint sound as the restless Hypsilophodons moved.

Suddenly there was a whooshing sound. It startled all the Hypsilophodons. They looked at each other, disturbed by the sudden noise. They tried to get closer to the rock for protection. The sound carried around the rock. The young creatures were seized with fear. The sound came from the wind which was sweeping across the rock and tree strewn plain. It increased in force, reaching a high level as it swept around the rock. The Hypsilophodons moved closer together to get away from this new torment.

Almost at the same time as the wind came up, the dawn was beginning to break. A faint light crept over the plains. Now the Hypsilophodons needed to be on their guard. There were some vicious creatures around and they would soon be out looking for their food.

The group of Hypsilophodons had a young male for a leader. He peered out from behind the rock. In the distance he could see the large forms of Iguanodons feeding on the fern-like vegetation.

The urge to feed was great. The Hypsilophodons had only eaten occasionally. Each time they had stopped they had been forced to move again because of the threat from Megalosaurus. In spite of their speed Hypsilophodons were often caught and eaten by these ferocious creatures.

The young male Hypsilophodon indicated to the others that it was time to leave. He moved slowly at first, and they followed him. Soon the group was bounding across the plain, easily avoiding the boulders.

The leader stopped by a shrub laden with ripe berries. Soon all the Hypsilophodons were feeding eagerly. For the first time in days they were able to eat without disturbance.

Suddenly the ground started to shudder. The group stopped feeding. Panic struck. They fled in all directions. They sought refuge behind anything they could find. Their panic was unnecessary. The disturbance had been caused by the approach of several Polacanthus. Like Iguanodons and Hypsilophodons, Polacanthus were also plant-eaters. They too had spotted the luscious berries.

The Hypsilophodons stayed hidden for some time. The leader, realizing that it was a false alarm, looked out from behind the tree trunk where he had taken cover. He called gently, a call which told the others that all was well.

They came out from their hiding places and assembled around the leader. He waited, realizing that not all the group had returned. In the distance he could see the form of a Hypsilophodon making its way slowly toward the group.

The leader left the others and made his way quickly to the distant creature. It soon became obvious what the problem was. In making for safety a young female Hypsilophodon had damaged a leg. She was limping badly. The male stayed with her as she made her way to the rest of the group. They eventually rejoined the others.

The young male leader led the female to a rock. By a series of vocal sounds, a young male was assigned to look after the injured female. Another male was to gather food and take it back to the two Hypsilophodons sheltering behind the rock.

The rest of the group made their way to shrubs laden with berries. This time they were more cautious. Members took turns guarding and warning the others if danger threatened.

Several large Pteranodons flew low over the plain. They were no threat to the Hypsilophodons. However, the creatures did not know this. They scattered, making for the nearest shelters. After the Pteranodons had gone they came out and regrouped to continue their feeding.

Suddenly the still air was shattered by the sound
of terrible cries. The Hypsilophodons stopped feeding.
They looked across the plain, not sure of where the
noise was coming from. Some distance away were three
Iguanodons. Two were engaged in battle. Two males
were fighting over the same female.

The young Hypsilophodons were anxious to see what was happening. They moved closer to the scene of the action. The Iguanodons relied on their strength when fighting.

When the first Hypsilophodons arrived at the site of the conflict the two Iguanodons were going around in circles. Neither seemed to be winning the contest.

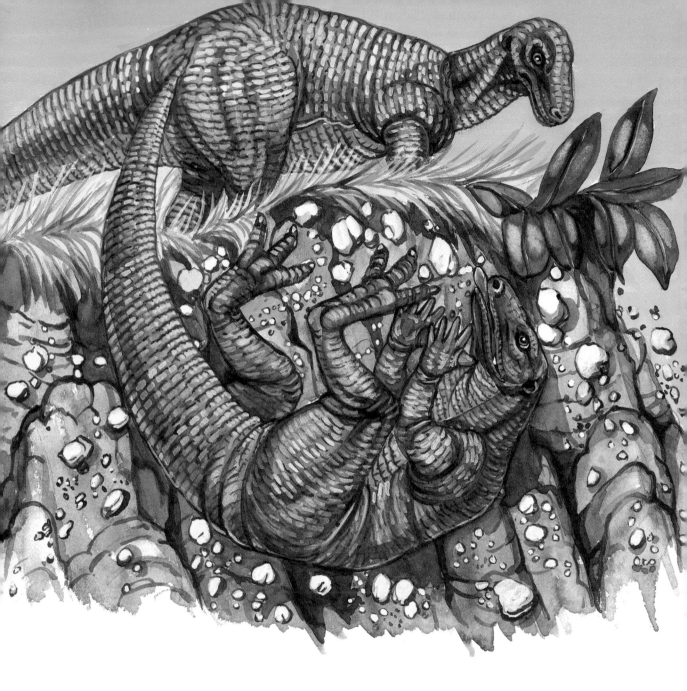

Suddenly there was a piercing shriek and the action was over. One Iguanodon plunged to its death over a cliff. The victor looked over the edge. Then he turned to the female and they continued to feed as if nothing had happened.

With nothing more to see the Hypsilophodons returned to their feeding activities. They had found a bush filled with berries some 150 feet from the two resting Hypsilophodons. At first they were ever on the lookout for danger. Gradually they all became so engrossed in satisfying their hunger that they forgot about their enemies.

A short, sharp cry of terror made the Hypsilophodons look up from their meal. The sound came from the rocks. They saw the reason for the anguished cry. A pair of Megalosaurus had crept up on the two Hypsilophodons. Now the young dinosaurs stood little chance. Soon they were in the grip of these powerful flesh-eaters. Faint cries of terror reached the other Hypsilophodons. They were rooted to the spot. The leader realized that there was little they could do to save two of their kind. At a signal from him the rest of the group made off as fast as their long, powerful legs would carry them.

The two unfortunate Hypsilophodons struggled. However, their efforts were in vain. They were no match for the much larger and more powerful Megalosaurus. It didn't take long for the creatures to eat their fill.

Meanwhile the fleeing Hypsilophodons had found shelter behind a large rocky outcrop. This was far enough from the scene of the attack. They rested here. Soon they would have to go off again to seek yet more food and face the ever present danger from their flesh-eating enemies.

Interesting facts about . . .
Hypsilophodon

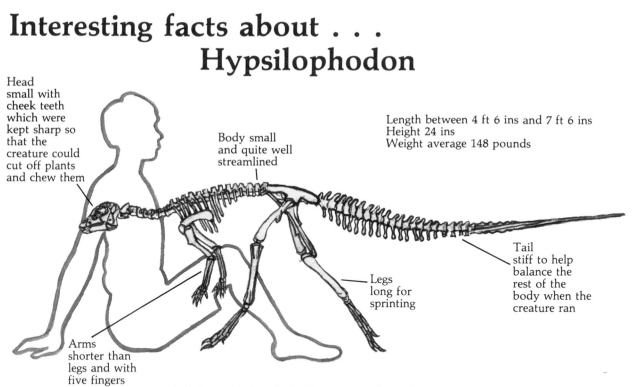

Head small with cheek teeth which were kept sharp so that the creature could cut off plants and chew them

Body small and quite well streamlined

Length between 4 ft 6 ins and 7 ft 6 ins
Height 24 ins
Weight average 148 pounds

Tail stiff to help balance the rest of the body when the creature ran

Legs long for sprinting

Arms shorter than legs and with five fingers

A skeleton of Hypsilophodon compared to a human

Dinosaurs are grouped into two orders. These are the Saurischian dinosaurs and the Ornithischian dinosaurs. Ornithoscian means "bird-hipped". These dinosaurs got their name because their hip bones are arranged like those of birds. The two orders are then divided up into a number of sub-orders. These include the Ornithopods, which means "bird-footed."

Ornithopods were the only group of Ornithischian dinosaurs which could walk or run on their hind legs.

We can compare ornithopods with some animals which live today. Deer take their food in a similar way. They pull leaves off trees. The bird-hipped dinosaurs took food like this.

Hypsilophodon was one of the smaller bird-hipped dinosaurs. In fact Hypsilophodontids didn't weigh as much as an average man (168 pounds).

Bird-hipped Dinosaurs
Hypsilophodon was one of a group of dinosaurs which belonged to a family called Hypsilophodontids. The name Hypsilophodontids means "high ridge teeth". It tells us about the food which the dinosaurs ate.

There were many different kinds of bird-hipped dinosaurs. Although Hypsilophodon was a small dinosaur, it could move very quickly. Its speed helped it to get away from its enemies. When a Hypsilophodon was running quickly its head,

body and tail were all in a straight line. It had to stop sometimes. Then its head was held up in much the same way as a bird holds its head.

One of the fastest creatures
Much work has been carried out on the remains of Hypsilophodons. Although scientists can't be certain, they do believe that it was one of the fastest creatures ever to live on the earth.

When did Hypsilophodon appear?
Hypsilophodon probably appeared at the beginning of the Age of Dinosaurs. This was 200 million years ago. The creature died out at the end of the Age of Dinosaurs, 135 million years later.

Did Hypsilophodon live in trees?
When the remains of the first Hypsilophodons were looked at it was thought that the dinosaur lived in trees. This was because of the way in which the toes were arranged. The largest of the toes appeared to be at a different angle to the other three. This arrangement was compared to the toes of birds. They thought that Hypsilophodon used its toes to hold on to branches.

Later, when more toes were looked at, it was found that they were parallel.

Fast mover on land
Far from being a creature which lived in trees, Hypsilophodon was found to be a fast mover on

land. If you look at the skeleton you will see that the bones of the lower leg are very long. All creatures which run quickly have long lower leg bones.

Hypsilophodon's tail was also special. It used its tail for balancing. When the dinosaur was moving quickly its tail kept it stable. Running at fast speeds it also had to avoid obstacles. The tail helped it to turn quickly in all directions.

What did Hypsilophodon eat?
All the bird-hipped dinosaurs ate plants. They all had special teeth. These had ridges on them. It was these ridged teeth which helped Hypsilophodon and the other bird-hipped dinosaurs to crush and grind the seeds and fruits which they ate.

Hypsilophodon had a horny beak. The beak was used to bite off pieces of plants. Inside the beak there was a row of small teeth in the upper part of the mouth. None of the other bird-hipped dinosaurs had small teeth like these. No one has been able to discover their function.

Other bird-hipped Dinosaurs
Some people find it strange that Hypsilophodon and Iguanodon were both bird-hipped dinosaurs. Unlike Hypsilophodon, Iguanodon was very large. It was 16 feet tall and 36 feet long. Whereas Hypsilophodon weighed about 140 pounds, Iguanodon weighed 4.5 tons (9,000 lbs.). You could have put 61 Hypsilophodons inside an Iguanodon!

Things to do

Find out the names of as many bird-hipped dinosaurs as you can. Look up the names of fast moving animals which are alive today. Try to find pictures of skeletons of these creatures. Look at the leg bones and compare them with those of Hypsilophodon.

Draw a picture of yourself and of Hypsilophodon to scale. Which is the biggest?

Try to find the names of other creatures living today which are about the same size as Hypsilophodon.

Make a model of Hypsilophodon. Use pipe cleaners or wire, and cover the skeleton with paper mache.

Make a long picture to go on the wall. Draw in a scene from the book. Paint it. Cut out as many different bird-hipped dinosaurs as you can. Then color your pictures and stick them on your wall picture.

All three creatures belonged to a group called Ornithopods, which means bird-footed. Iguanodon was large. Large numbers of these creatures have been found. Hypsilophodon was fleet of foot. All three creatures were browsers.

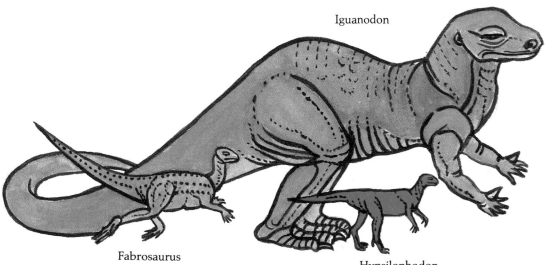

Iguanodon

Fabrosaurus

Hypsilophodon